overcoming overthinking: Guide to building a healthy relationship

Noble Justice

Table of contents

Chapter 1

What constitutes overthinking in a relationship

The fact is that everyone overthinks things from time to time. In my counseling practice, it is one of the most prevalent problems I deal with. People commonly come in for their visits stating things like, "I can't relax. It's like my head won't shut off," or, "I can't stop thinking about how my life may have been better if I'd have done things differently."

The act of overthinking may be connected to psychological disorders such as anxiety and depression, but it's impossible to determine which arises first in each person. It's kind of like a "chicken or egg" type problem. Either way, it's evident that overthinking may cause your mental health to suffer. And then when mental health worsens, it becomes more and more tempting to overthink. It's like a violent downward spiral.

It’s hard to detect while right in the thick of it, though. It’s easy to persuade oneself that pondering and fretting about things is somehow useful. After all, how is it possible to come up with a better solution without thinking about it? You have to constantly think about that mistake to avoid yourself from repeating it, right? Well, the solution is not as apparent as you may expect.

“Analysis paralysis” is genuine. The more you think about a situation, the worse you feel. And the worse you feel, the harder it is to take effective action since emotions may obscure your judgment.

Two Types of Overthinking

Overthinking generally entails brooding on the past and fretting about the future.

Overthinking isn't the same as good problem-solving. Problem-solving consists of thinking about a challenging scenario when required. Overthinking, on the other side, includes lingering on the issue.

Overthinking is also distinct from self-reflection. Self-reflection may be good since it entails learning and gaining perspective on yourself about the circumstance at hand. It is also deliberate. Overthinking, though, is thinking about everything you don't have control over, and then obsessing on how horrible you feel about it. It does not assist generate any understanding of the problem.

The amount of time you spend in deep thinking doesn't important, however. If any amount of time is spent genuinely learning from prior behavior and coming up with innovative alternatives, then it is productive. But time spent overthinking won't enrich your life at all, regardless of whether it's 10 minutes or 10 hours.

Signs You're Overthinking Right Now

Before you can improve your thinking patterns, you have to become aware of when you're overthinking.

Here are 10 warning signals that you're overthinking:

- I can't stop worrying.
- I frequently worry about things I have no control over.
- I continually remind myself of errors.
- I replay humiliating incidents in my thoughts over and again.
- I regularly ask myself "what if..." questions.
- I have difficulties sleeping because it seems like my brain won't shut down.
- When I recollect discussions with someone, I can't help but think about

all the things I wish I had or hadn't said.

- I spend a lot of leisure time wondering about the hidden meaning behind things people say or situations that occur.
- When someone says something or behaves in a manner I don't like, I linger on it.
- I spend so much time either concentrating on previous events or worrying about the future that I frequently overlook what's going on in the now.

It could seem like you're the only one laying awake at night, lingering on a choice you made earlier that day or fretting about tomorrow's to-do list. But you're not alone. In many circumstances, overthinking might show itself as rumination, which commonly entails perseverating on events of the past and even the present with a negative perspective. Whether your habit of overthinking leads you into the past or focuses on the future, there are constructive strategies to reframe your ideas and worry less.

While overthinking itself is not a mental disease, it is related to problems like depression, anxiety, eating disorders, and drug use disorders. Rumination may be frequent in persons who have chronic pain and chronic sickness as well, taking the shape of negative thoughts about that discomfort and recovery from it.

The first step to avoiding overthinking in your relationship is to begin exploring why you feel the impulse to overthink in the first place. One of the unique traits of humans is that we can think about and examine our thoughts and emotions.

Overthinking Is How You Learned To Cope

When we feel worried, our body instinctively installs coping methods to lessen the perceived risk. In the case of partnerships, being deeply involved in a certain result for a relationship yet feeling doubtful of a good conclusion, may cause overwhelming sensations. You may be adopting overthinking as a means to take control and reduce the worry that this unknown scenario causes.

Overthinking Is Rooted In Control

Other ways of thinking and acting may make life simpler and some can make life more difficult. One thought pattern that might generate stress in your life is the assumption that you can influence certain occurrences external to yourself.

You would undoubtedly agree that it's ridiculous to suppose you can control the weather. But many individuals who overthink feel they can influence what their partner chooses to do (and the results of the relationship) by hyper-analyzing certain areas of the relationship.

Believing we can control situations that are not genuinely within our control is a recipe for worry. We want to have an overall picture of how to quit overthinking in a relationship. To avoid overthinking in relationships, it's necessary to recognize and accept the things that are and are not in your locus (or region) of control.

For Example: Suppose your spouse isn't very excellent at answering their phone or replying to texts in a timely way. When they don't react after a few hours, it starts to make you fear that they are leaving you, or that they don't care anymore.

In instances like these, it may be good to bring out a piece of paper and write down what you can and cannot manage.

You CAN'T force your spouse to reply more rapidly. You also CAN'T make them remember to charge their phone at the nights so it's not dead when you contact them.

But you CAN take charge of your emotions and install new techniques to help you manage more efficiently when you are feeling nervous. And you CAN discuss your thoughts with your spouse and urge that they reply more rapidly in the future.

Chapter 2

The consequences of overthinking.

Overthinking may seem innocent, but it may have a detrimental influence on your mental and physical health. Here's how you can cope with it.

Have you ever caught yourself pondering much too much and not accomplishing anything? Do you frequently find yourself lingering over a specific topic? Are you continuously concerned, with your mind racing all the time? This is what we call a tendency of overthinking, which does nothing else but ruins us and our mental tranquility.

Most of us pay attention to various things from time to time, but some of us immerse ourselves in a loop of thinking that keeps us occupied but in a bad way. This vicious loop goes on repeating itself and invading good habits. Overcoming overthinking is a skill that is not mastered by many, but has to be practiced at the earliest to stop the negative cycle.

The difficulties of overthinking extend to all sectors of life. The time that must be spent thinking about anything useful and attentive is frequently utilized in self-limiting and not self-reflecting, self-awareness, and progress. This has a harmful influence not just on mental health but on emotional and physical health as well. The frequent patterns of overthinking may lead to worry, impatience, panic attacks as well as poor appetite, inconsistent sleep patterns, high blood pressure, and much more. Emotions have a vital part when it comes to keeping oneself sane.

The objective should be to fool the brain to quit worrying and overthinking.
Why overthinking is bad?
Overthinking is more than just an annoyance — research suggests that

thinking too much may have a toll on your overall well-being too.

Here is how overthinking may affect you:

May trigger mental illness

Are you continually concentrating on your previous mistakes? Dwelling on your faults, troubles, and failings raises your chances of being impacted by mental health issues. Overthinking may set you up for a vicious loop that is hard to stop. It wreaks havoc on your mental tranquility and when you lose your peace of mind, you tend to overthink.

Interferes with problem-solving capacity

Do you overanalyze things? Overthinkers feel that repeating specific circumstances or difficulties in the brain helps them overcome them. However, research indicates differently. Overanalyzing interferes with one's capacity to solve issues since it drives you to concentrate on the problem and envisage circumstances that may never exist, rather than finding a solution.

Even making basic decisions, like picking an outfit for the day or deciding on the next vacation site, may seem like a life-or-death issue when you are an overthinker. Ironically, all that overthinking will never help you make a better decision!

Disrupts your sleep

If you are an overthinker, you probably suffer sleep troubles. This is because your body does not enable you to sleep when your mind is not at rest. Ruminating on practically everything and fretting incessantly about things over which you have little or no control sometimes lead to fewer hours of sleep. Thus, overthinking lowers your quality of sleep and may make you grumpy the following day as well.

Overthinking might make you anticipate bad implications and leap to erroneous conclusions. This might certainly lead to disagreements with your spouse who can feel unhappy for being misunderstood practically every time.

You struggle to connect

Obsessing over tiny things and events may damage your mood and impair your self-esteem. Even your lover might sense your persistent anxiousness and pain at times. You can end up not being in sync with your actual feelings and struggle to develop a meaningful relationship with someone.

10 Ways Overthinking Ruins Relationships

Apart from the impact overthinking has on you, it may also influence your relationship. Here are 10 ways overthinking destroys your relationship.

1. ***Your skepticism destroys the connection***

Since pessimism is your closest companion right now, nice things seldom attract your attention. So your spouse, whom you have known for some time now, suddenly becomes a possible cheater and a liar in your thoughts.

Even if they try their greatest best and leave no reason for you to question, you cannot help but continually assume the worst and you even believe they are constantly lying in the relationship.

Your persistent skepticism becomes unpleasant for your spouse who finally could desire a way out of the relationship. So there you go your overthinking might wreck your relationship

2. ***You fully lose yourself in the process of overthinking***
With all the overthinking, you are hardly the same person anymore. You could confront your spouse about something, and have emotional outbursts over what you believe is going on.

After a few months, you have become a permanently anxious, depressed person who starts up arguments over trivial things. The person you have become scares you as much yet you are unable to cease becoming that.

3. ***Everything is on the extremity of the spectrum***
Nothing has a middle ground. No regular explanation works for you. They have to be on the extreme extremes of the reason spectrum.

As we discussed before your overthinking methods drive you to high imagining heights. Whether your spouse left on a business trip you keep wondering if he's having fun with a female colleague while he is working hard and picking up presents for you.

Imagine his position when he arrives home and you continuously accuse him of cheating and emotionally ignoring you since you are now on the verge of overthinking. Your reply puts a foul taste in his mouth and he feels horrible. It causes a split in the connection that's hard to reconcile.

4. ***You are continuously paranoid***

The lack of trust paired with overthinking causes you to feel worried that someone is barging into your connection. Obsessive-compulsive conduct of knowing where your lover is every minute of the day is you becoming paranoid.

You even keep wondering, "Is he cheating or am I paranoid?" But you can scarcely manage your own emotions and you keep disappearing into the dark hole of overthinking.

You also constantly thinking about accidents, horrible illnesses and fires, and tragedies impacting your family. You believe your paranoia is keeping them safe but you are damaging them beyond control.

5. ***No solutions, more difficulties***

Since no logical justification is good enough, since you will always find a way around it, you come up with odd excuses to justify the reason presented. You don't have any answer to your difficulties; only a massive pile of additional absurd problems.

It becomes a misery to live with you and you fail to understand that overthinking is harming your relationship. The continual tension you experience you pass it on to your family. You accentuate the issues and never search for a solution.

6. ***Trust is gone from the relationship***
In the process of thinking about things and being a pessimist, trust is entirely gone from the relationship. Paranoia could lead to conflicts which might generate a further gap in communication.

Overthinking generally pops up when trust is lost in a relationship. If you have cause to suspect your spouse is not to be trusted, losing your peace of mind won't assist anybody. In the middle of all this negative thinking, re-thinking, and overthinking, trust difficulties keep hurting the partnership.

Communication is a cornerstone of a good relationship. One could attempt to share all the things one has in their brain, simply to vent it out and a faithful partner would understand.

7. ***You experience anxiety concerns***
Overthinking does contribute to anxiety difficulties. You are always worried and you acquire patterns like double texting. You become highly agitated when your spouse or your children don't contact you promptly and true to your nature you start fearing the worse.

This is how overthinking damages your relationship and your spouse believes you are always pursuing them keeping a watch on their whereabouts.

8. ***Your quiet overthinking is behaving like a slow poison***
When you are overthinking you may not speak it constantly but your behaviors begin acting like a gradual poison on the relationship. Overthinking may make you domineering and manipulative because you want things to go your way.

If things don't go the way you want them to you feel nervous. So you do your absolute best to keep every scenario under your control and it makes your spouse utterly claustrophobic.

9. *It takes away all the enjoyment from the relationship*

When was the last time you felt extremely pleased and relaxed? You spend a day with your lover without worrying that things might go wrong? Overthinking in relationships might be destroying it completely since you are never in a comfortable frame of mind.

You keep wondering how to make my wife happy but you end up being so tense and stressed that happiness becomes an illusion in your relationship.

10. ***Your partner begins searching for a way out***

Your overthinking becomes such a problem in your relationship that your spouse feels the noose tightening around their neck gradually.

Can you picture how your partner's life is with someone, who is continuously uneasy, and worried, amplifies any tiny event to the worst case conceivable, and continues nagging about that?

Naturally, your spouse would search for a way out of such a relationship. Once they are gone you will recognize how overthinking has destroyed your connection.

Chapter 3

What causes individuals to overthink in a relationship.

Overthinking Is Rooted In Insecurity

Overthinking in a relationship typically has its origins in your history. There was most certainly someone you genuinely cared for but the relationship didn't turn out the way you wanted.

You may not have understood why the relationship broke and you may have felt abandoned. You may have suffered a deep level of sadness, loneliness, or suffering over the death of this individual.

You might get overwhelmed with the notion of the relationship abruptly ending in a similar fashion to your former experience. This leads to an effort to limit the risk of this occurring by overanalyzing.

However, when you attempt to control every area of a connection, it may frequently make your partner feel overwhelmed and claustrophobic. This might really wind up driving them away, bringing about the same predicament you had sought to avoid.

A root fear

Overthinking arises from a certain insecurity or fundamental worry. This insecurity may come from childhood, a former relationship, or overall poor self-esteem or trust difficulties.

Excess time or energy

When you have a lot of spare time or energy, you may find yourself overthinking or chewing over relationship advice to pass the time.

Lack of trust

If your relationship lacks a foundation of trust, you may feel unable to accept what your spouse tells you, prompting you to overthink their behaviors and replies.

Lack of communication

when each partner fails to be honest or transparent about their emotions or behaviors, you may begin to overthink to fill in the holes in your communication.

In virtually every scenario, you're worrying about an incident or encounter that went down with another individual. I mean, how often do you pause to dwell on something that you did while no one else was around? Probably never. Overthinking is usually always in connection to someone else, as you have no conceivable means of knowing what another person is thinking at any particular moment. Overthinking may happen with colleagues, employers, family members, friends, strangers—anyone, really—but it most commonly happens (or at least, you notice it most) with reference to a love interest or partner. You see, thinking about someone you like is a method of staying near to them, of, quite literally, having them on your mind. Then when a discussion or event comes along that, for whatever reason, leaves you unclear of how they feel about you or your relationship, you go into "find it out" mode as a means to take control.

Yep, it's generally a control problem. Let's imagine a man suddenly begins contacting you less regularly, or a female you're digging hasn't initiated a third date, much to your surprise. You start replaying everything that you said on your previous date, rereading texts, attempting to find hidden meaning in anything they've done or haven't done, all in an effort to link their shift in behavior or lack of participation to a single point.

Because if you're able to "figure things out," then you're able to "fix it." Or, at least, so it appears. Truth is, in most circumstances, you'll never truly know why someone didn't go further with you, and even if you somehow do, it's generally not something that can be "fixed."

How to tell when you are thinking too much.

Thinking about all the things you might have done differently, second-guessing every choice you make, and contemplating all the worst-case possibilities in life can be taxing. But, overthinking is a hard habit to quit.

You could even persuade yourself that thinking about something for a tremendously long period is the key to producing the greatest answer, but that's typically not the case.

In fact, the longer you think about something, the less time and energy you may have to take meaningful action.

Of course, everyone overthinks occasionally. Maybe you keep worrying about all the things that may go wrong when you make a presentation next week.

Maybe you've spent endless hours trying to select what to wear to that job interview and as a consequence, you didn't spend any time preparing your responses.

Before you can put a stop to overthinking, you have to realize when you're doing it. Here's how to detect when you're overthinking.

You're Not Solution-Focused

Overthinking is distinct from problem-solving. Overthinking is about concentrating on the issue, whereas problem-solving entails seeking for a solution.

Imagine a storm is approaching. Here's the difference between overthinking and problem-solving:

Overthinking: "I hope the storm wouldn't arrive. It's going to be dreadful. I hope the home doesn't get harmed. Why do these things constantly have to happen to me? I can't handle this."

Problem-solving: "I will go outside and pick up anything that could blow away. I'll lay sandbags against the garage door to avoid flooding. If we have a lot of rain I'll go to the market to get plywood so I can board up the windows."

Problem-solving may lead to beneficial action. Overthinking, on the other hand, promotes unpleasant feelings and doesn't explore for answers.

You Experience Repetitive Thoughts

Ruminating—or repeating the same things over and over again—isn't useful. But, when you're overthinking, you can find yourself rehearsing a discussion in your brain again or visualizing something horrible occurring numerous times.

Dwelling on your difficulties, failures, and weaknesses, raises your chance of mental health issues, according to a 2013 research published in the Journal of Abnormal Psychology. As your mental health suffers, you are more likely you are to dwell on your thoughts. It's a recurring loop that may be challenging to stop.

Your Worrying Keeps You Up at Night

When you're overthinking you could feel like your brain won't shut down. When you attempt to sleep, you could even feel as if your brain is on overdrive as it repeats scenes in your mind and leads you to picture horrible things occurring.

Research verifies what you presumably already know—rumination interferes with sleep. Overthinking makes it difficult to fall asleep.

Overthinking lowers the quality of your sleep too. So it's difficult to get into a deep sleep when your brain is busy overthinking everything.

Difficulty falling asleep may add to more worried thoughts. For example, when you don't fall asleep straight away, you can assume that you'll be overtired the next day. That may lead you to feel anxious—which may make it much difficult to fall asleep.

You Struggle to Make Decisions

You can attempt to persuade yourself that thinking longer and harder benefits you. After all, you're looking at an issue from every feasible perspective. But, overanalyzing and fretting really creates a barrier. Research reveals pondering too much makes it challenging to make judgments. If you're undecided about everything from what to eat for dinner to which hotel you should book, you could be overthinking things.

It's extremely probable that you are spending a lot of time seeking for second views and analyzing your alternatives, but eventually, those tiny decisions may not matter that much.

You Second Guess Decisions

Overthinking sometimes means beating yourself up for the choices you previously made.

You may spend a lot of time believing your life would be better if you'd just chosen that other job or not established a company. Or maybe you become irritated with yourself for not recognizing red flags sooner—because you think they should have been evident!

And although a little healthy self-reflection might help you learn from your errors, reliving and second-guessing is a type of mental agony.

Overthinking may take a toll on your mood and may make it much more difficult to make choices in the future.

You constantly want to discover the why behind everything

The word, 'why', has led to so many discoveries throughout history. It drives what we do and our emotional responses to things. We scarcely need to ask why. But... I know you were anticipating the but, it is virtually not possible to know the 'why' behind anything. This might lead to a vicious loop of thinking that doesn't help you feel any better.

Most of the time you second doubt yourself and choices

Recently, I saw this on psychology today "...second-guess in time saves nine". Truth is, taking a second action from a previously thought idea has its own perks. However, doing this all the time so it gets more and more difficult to make a conclusion is an indication you are overthinking.

You spend too much time making a choice or decision
Still building on the preceding symbol, envision this cycle. Just as soon as you thought of anything, you second-guess, alter the plan of action, second-guess then change it again, usually to the initial choice and this continues on. You would undoubtedly spend considerably more time making a choice. This is a warning indicating you are overthinking

You have problems sleeping or focusing
Our brain may function on autopilot, providing us the capacity to accomplish activities swiftly, automatically. This applies even to overthinking. So, even when you would prefer sleep or focus, your mind continues running round and round. Our brain learn to autopilot after we have done a

job over a couple of times, in this example, overthinking.

If you believe you are overthinking, you probably are\sUnderstanding what defines overthinking is not as clear as ABC.

Some few weeks ago, I asked a Vet doctor in Lagos, Nigeria, who is is also a friend, how to recognize when my gorgeous seven months old Rott was shedding "too much". His reaction was quite obvious "If the owner believes a dog is shedding too much, they usually are". While I was hoping for some professional recommendations, this pierced through since this is one of the main signs for a mental health battle for us. If a person feels there is a mental health challenge, there usually is.

I put this sign as the final since it sort of covers every point presented so far, and anybody not mentioned here. So the next time you are overthinking, take real measures to identify and address.

Chapter 4

Fixing overthinking in a relationship.

Reframe the mental process and notice the snowball effect before it becomes an avalanche

Overthinking is like watching your ideas roll down a slope and get larger and bigger. Healthy thinking patterns would provide you the means to avoid the snowball effect, but in an anxious brain, the "brakes" may become a bit defective.

When you can't stop the flow of "what-ifs" or you're belaboring a point or a problem over and again, people closest around you may start to feel it, too.

Give it a name, give it a definite time, and reframe it

One method to press pause on the snowball effect is to call it out. Name what's happening: "I'm over-thinking."

Once you've called it out, give it a certain period. You may let the thinking process continue for 1 minute, for example, and then move on once you have given it a name and given it time. Set a timer for it.

Then, attempt to redirect your concentration on something actionable and real, something outside of your thoughts, like the meal in front of you, your partner's speech, or the music surrounding you if you're out. Reframe the thinking pattern to assist shift your attention to the present and your surroundings.

Do something exciting with your partner

workout, walk or arrange a vacation. If you feel yourself slipping into analysis paralysis or pondering too deeply over what your spouse said, apply the aforementioned approach, and then consider changing your landscape. Go for a stroll around the block with your companion and speak about your favorite recent novels or movies.

Plan a trek or a weekend excursion; the planning phase will put your brain to work in a proactive manner that will benefit both you and your spouse well. Don't be scared to make errors in your preparation or in the activities you pick.

When you own your choices and allow yourself to see that "wrong decisions" are chances to learn or opportunities to try something new and unexpected, you'll find the things you do together and your time together will be more rewarding.

Give yourself a chance to notice the overthinking habits and what causes them Ultimately, it's all about reframing the mental process and spotting the snowball effect before that snowball becomes an avalanche. Give yourself a chance to notice the overthinking habits and what prompts them. Write it down.

Discuss it with your spouse so they can help you halt it in its tracks, too

Find assistance with a local therapist who can help you analyze your thinking patterns and behaviors
Find assistance with a local therapist who can help you investigate your thinking patterns and behaviors, preferably using methods like cognitive behavioral therapy that are meant to provide you with practical skills to help reframe negative thought patterns into positive ones.

Let's swap the phrase overthinking with obsessing.

Think of the obsessive mind as an agitated rat in a cage running round and round without any purpose. Or picture a record with a scratch continuously stuck on the same lyric, “Does he love me, does he not?” There are no discoveries, no push toward action—merely questions without answers.

There is, however, one predicted effect of overthinking/obsessing:
Agitation.
The more your mind is concentrated on ideas that go nowhere and on questions that disguise your fear and fury, the more powerless and passive you will become.

Here are a few instances of questions without answers (overthinking/obsessing). Embedded beneath compulsive thought are unnamed sentiments of hatred, pain, and loneliness.

Why doesn’t she love me anymore?
Why doesn’t he ever ask me how I am?
Why does he want to spend more time with his buddies than with me?
Why isn’t she interested in sex anymore?

Note that the obsessive mind prefers to ask why inquiries. Questions starting with how or what tends to lead to answers, particularly if the inquiry focuses on the questioner's area of responsibility, such as "What can I do to show her I love her?"

To reiterate: if the conclusion of these why inquiries lead only to despair, then it's evidence of overthinking.

Let's contrast it with thinking. For our conversation, I'm defining thinking as problem-solving— asking the correct questions that lead toward a clear route of action.

Thinking (Problem Solving) (Problem Solving)

Imagine you're sleeping on a nice sandy beach thinking about your connection with your spouse. (Of course, you're well-protected with suntan lotion since you realize the expense of disregarding logical implications such as burning your skin.)

Your mind then wanders to a recent quarrel. You see yourself being quietly afraid and bewildered as your spouse urges you to be more truthful. What she sees is a strained, irritated expression on your face. She responds with rage at your apparent apathy and coldness.

Here on the beach, secure from confrontation and humiliation, your mind runs through a five-stage thinking process you heard from a relationship podcast:

Name it

You dig down deep, and you realize how afraid you are of being exposed. The emotion of terror is palpable for you. So is your rage. You comprehend how you increase dread into a rage. You may now give names to these sentiments.

Claim it

You recognize that your companion didn't make you terrified and furious. These are your responses, sensations, and emotions. You claim them as yours. As you advance through this second stage, you replace blame with accountability for your conduct. After all, they are your sentiments.

Tame it

On the beach, you imagine how reactive you were. Your reflecting self didn't show up for that interaction. You realize that when you miss phases 1 and 2, you may easily descend into defensiveness and blaming. It's not your best self.

Frame it

Right now, your reflective self is in command, and it's delving further.

It wants to understand why you're so terrified to disclose yourself. Why this protective response when your lover desires a deeper connection? To yourself, you may accept your fear of rejection—your worry that if she understood your weaknesses, she wouldn't want to be with you.

On the beach, you get an insight that you're ruled by a self-fulfilling prophecy: When you feel rejected, you respond in a rejecting manner.
The result: you receive what you dread most—rejection.

Aim it
You decide to take a risk to be real. You communicate your fear of rejection with your partner and apologize for your protective behavior. To your great surprise and relief, your lover replies with affection and understanding.

Because she understands you, she adds, "Don't worry, I love you much more knowing that even you may be vulnerable at times."

These stages are how you transition from overthinking to thinking. Healthy thinking leads to problem-solving. Overthinking leads to anxiety and apathy.

Relationships may be an incredible source of love and support. In truth, most individuals crave for a relationship and someone they have a connection with. We all want to feel important and know that we matter, particularly to someone we're in a relationship with.

While this is a reasonable desire, when we worry how much we mean to our partners or whether they're as involved in the relationship as we are, we tend to overthink and obsess over the state and health of the connection.

The overthinking we experience is all about fear and worry.

Ultimately we're worried that our connection is not as solid as we assume, and we're terrified of being let down and disappointed by our partners. This suggests we have issues inside the partnership and what it signifies for the future of the relationship. However, if we're overthinking, we're likely not communicating the way that we need to.

There are three stages to stopping the torment of overthinking:

Slow down and examine what's actually upsetting you about the connection
When we overthink, we are in a condition of emotional overflow. When we're feeling inundated, we are emotionally overwhelmed, and our thoughts begin to speed. When this occurs, we either shut down and don't say anything, or we begin to whine.

Complaining to our spouse does not alleviate our concerns or help them comprehend our position any differently. When we begin to find ourselves overthinking, we need to sit down first and analyze what is actually hurting us or worrying us out about the connection.

Many times we leap into complaining or repairing without fully grasping what we are worried and disturbed about.

Focus on communication

Once you dive into what you're thinking and feeling, the aim is to discuss your worries with your spouse. This is the moment to clearly, simply, and honestly explain what is in your heart—not the rushing thoughts that make you feel like you're spinning out of control.

To accomplish this, softly start the discussion by explaining how you feel without blaming or condemning your spouse.

Once you convey your problem, then follow up with what you need. When we do this, we are informing our partners what we're upset with and then proposing a remedy. Be open to hearing your partner's answer and any worries, so it's a good dialogue.

Trust the basis and durability of the relationship

Lastly, trust yourself. Many times we overthink in relationships because we are terrified of losing what we have. Our purpose is to defend it and safeguard it, but when we stress and overthink, we are effectively stifling the connection.

We are denying the relationship the opportunity to develop and flourish.

We have to trust the basis and stability of the connection we formed by allowing ourselves, our spouse, and our relationships opportunity to develop. When we believe in the base of the relationship, we give room to acquire and practice new abilities together.

And eventually, we have to believe that regardless of what occurs inside the relationship, that we are capable of managing it and making the right option for ourselves.

Overthinking in a relationship or in other circumstances is frequently based on anxiousness. Obviously, in problem-solving and decision-making, a certain level of cogitating is essential to develop good results and take care of oneself and others.

Overthinking, however, does not propel us ahead in relationships or encourage well-being. Paradoxically, it frequently deters us from both.

The greatest ways for avoiding overthinking include:

Understanding overthinking
Overthinking is a behavior formed in infancy because it was adaptive then, but it has become maladaptive today. Perhaps our childhood relationships were tumultuous, or we were abused and survived emotionally by thinking long and hard about every step we made.

If we analyzed every choice about how it would effect Mom or Dad, we probably lived better than if we'd just responded without anticipating how every possibility may play out. This method was beneficial to us back then, but today it merely gets us mired down in thinking or fearing the worst and keeps us immobilized from action.

Another reason we could overthink is if our parents were overly reactive and impulsive. We could have resolved never to be like them because of how harmful their lack of judgment was to them and us.

Instead, since they didn't give things much consideration, we could assume that giving things great thought is a superior method. The fact is that we desire a balance of thinking just enough.

Recognizing there's no "right" method

In relationships, we generally overthink to ensure we're doing the proper thing and avoid being hurt, as in embarrassed, rejected, or abandoned. But there is seldom a "right" thing to do in life since we don't know the future.

Instead, there's a "best" option to continue based on the present facts we have and our confidence about how our choice will effect the future.

Should we say yes to a second date with Jeff?

Should we marry Charlene?
Did Juan's flirting imply he doesn't love us?
What does it indicate that Shanika routinely cancels arrangements with us?

Getting comments from others

People go round and round in their thoughts thinking about what to do, and it never occurs to them to seek others for opinion. Maybe they're scared they'll look weak or dumb asking for assistance or don't trust other people.

If someone is contemplating about having a divorce, for example, the feedback of friends and family is typically quite useful. This is equally true for small exchanges in a relationship. Getting an outside viewpoint is preferable than recycling your own old thoughts in your brain.

Putting a deadline on a choice

We frequently overthink in lieu of making a choice because we fear saying or doing the "wrong" thing. The longer and deeper we ponder, the more we may postpone the eventual option. Overthinking merely gets us more stuck and enables more worry to build about determining what to do.

It's good to set ourselves a time period—a day or a week—to ponder our alternatives and not continue beyond that point unless we have fresh facts.

It's crucial to note that overthinking is not healthy as a regular problem-solving method and is often a sign of underlying anxiety or depression. Talking with a therapist is effective in overcoming relationship difficulties, either going alone or with someone.

Because therapists are impartial (unless when abuse or neglect is present) and have insight into mental health difficulties, they're not only useful in resolving knotty situations but in detecting underlying problems that generate overthinking and replacing them with healthier techniques.

Accept the reality that you and your spouse are two persons who are distinct in your own ways

When you meet someone exceptional, you may feel overexcited and become charmed by that person's charisma. You may start to ponder about every single element of the person's existence.

This appears to be acceptable up to a certain level only. However, if you start overthinking about the same person, start finding out what's happening in the other person's life, attempting to evaluate if both of you can make it up to a happy relationship or not, you may end up creating an imbalance in your personal life.

Overthinking may drive you to continually ponder over 'what if' circumstances. You will never be able to live in the moments of life. There will be no delight in the connection; rather, your major purpose will be solely to analyze the future of the partnership.

This may also lead to trust concerns, jealously, monitoring behaviors on the partner's varied places. You may also start thinking about some suspected cheats that may be entirely false.

The relationship may grow clinging and lose the much-needed distance that it needs.

Overthinking may also cause you to find out unneeded red flags in the relationship, most of which never truly exist. The troubles about which you may think are your anxieties and weaknesses becoming realized in the ideas.

Overthinking will never lead to a happy relationship. It occurs because your ideas are not founded on proof; it's your invention that does not link to any genuine real-life validation. Thus, overthinking is a hallmark of relationship uneasiness, leading to an abrupt and premature termination of the link permanently.

Some ways to stop overthinking are:

Communicate properly with your partner and fix the difficulties, if any. It assists in better expressing yourself to your spouse and know each other well. You only need to open yourself and see things plainly and simply as far as possible.
Accept the idea that you and your spouse are two people, thus each of you is distinct in their own ways. You will not be able to control everything they say or do. Just have patience and learn to let go of things that you do not like. If you know how to avoid things that hurt, you will have no space to ponder too much about the matter.
Learn to view things as simple as possible. Never attempt to complicate matters by

trying to ferret out hidden meanings behind every phrase or behavior of your spouse. This will assist to reduce jealousy and distrust in the relationship.

Overthinking arises if you sit inactively and do not concentrate your attention on some constructive activity. Thus, attempt to conduct some creative job or follow your lost pastime. If you stay involved, you will not overthink.

Try to erase your uncertainties and innermost worries since, in most instances, it is transferred in the relationship and makes you think a lot about it. You may eradicate your fundamental anxieties by repairing your wounded self-esteem. You only need an additional dose of self-confidence to recognize yourself as worthy. You will never need your spouse to tell you that you're good enough. Focus on your strengths and think about all the positive attributes you have. If you do not need to prove yourself to your lover, you will be more assured about the future of your relationship. You and your lover will accept each other with all the faults and defects.

If you suspect that there are trust concerns, you may speak to a confidant of yours to obtain a different view regarding the matter. It might be a close friend, a coworker, or maybe your parent as well. If you are living alone with your ideas, you may overthink, but if you discuss your issues with others, it will enable you to view things from a new perspective. You will have additional ideas to cope with the situation.

Seek treatment from a professional therapist if overthinking is taking a toll on your mental health.

You should avoid monitoring phone messages and social media updates every now and then. Do not attempt to overanalyze the tone and substance of the message and dwell with it for hours.

Practice mindfulness actively by concentrating your thoughts on the present moment. You may meditate or read an engaging book. Focus on things that matter.

Try to keep yourself mentally active all the time to prevent getting dominated by unreasonable ideas.

"Overthinking is gradual poisoning. It shatters you down before you even notice the loss."

Most of us feel nervous about our relationships. We push our cognitive process to another level by letting any small concerns touch our nerves. Are you someone or, do you know someone who overthinks in a relationship? Give it a read to assist yourself.

Do not allow anybody to enter your personal space and it goes the same for you
Do not allow anybody to breach your personal space and, it goes the same for you. Every person has the grace to build up their comfort bubble around themselves. Nothing like a relationship enables someone to break off that bubble.

When one respects the personal space of both parties, a relationship will be simpler to keep on.

Limit digital interaction

Do you aware that 50% of the talks are misconceived via texts? Define limits for connections so they may go light on your thoughts.

Do prefer one-on-one chats and meets; it will ensure that they are willing to take out time to see you. Waiting for the spouse to react is taxing and disheartening. Text them and move on.

Take pride to have the luxury of self-respect

Take pride to have the luxury of self-respect, and don't allow continual pondering to undermine your confidence. The instant you conceive of yourself as equal to them, you won't overthink topics that are not worth the energy and attention.

Pamper yourself and emphasize self-care

Be your employer and analyze your activity. Check out the red signs of compulsive love or connection to your relationship. Get occupied with things you enjoy. Pamper yourself and emphasize self-care. Give focus on your work instead of worrying about why your significant other said or did something that they scarcely recall today.

Allow the benefit of the doubt to your spouse

Assumptions damage your instincts. Nourish your instincts attentively however, don't assume anything before being definite about them. Get to discover the depth of issues. Give yourself time. Allow the benefit of the doubt to your companion. It's probable that what is squeezing your thoughts must be a random deed for them. Understand the power of tales and perspective.

Relationships are created quickly, but it takes a lot from two people to sustain the charm.

Live in the now. Past is the memory and, the future is fantasy. All we have on hand is the present moment. Live life to the fullest, and do not overthink anything.

You need to instruct your brain to cease over-analyzing

If you're an over-thinker, you may be acquainted with the phrase "analysis paralysis." When you have analysis paralysis, it indicates that you are immobilized and unable to go on because you are over-analyzing the circumstance.

This is absolutely not where you want to be in a love relationship.

Don't repeat discussions in your brain

In order to quit over-thinking in a relationship, you need to teach your brain to stop over-analyzing the relationship. Don't re-read text messages or repeat conversations in your brain. Replaying what has occurred in the past is not useful.

Practice remaining in the present moment
On the contrary, pondering too much about the future might also be harmful.

When you overthink the future of your relationship, you will place unneeded pressure on yourself and your spouse. Over-thinking the future may sometimes contribute to emotions of uncertainty and worry. Instead, try remaining in the current moment.

When you are with your lover, concentrate on enjoying the time you spend together rather than obsessing about what it implies. Enjoy the current time! Relationships vary with time, so embrace the stage of your relationship that you are now in.

Understand your attachment type and the attachment style of your spouse

If you truly want to quit your over-thinking habit once and for all, you need to understand where it's coming from. This conduct often arises from insecurity, general worry, or concerns of abandonment. Working with a qualified therapist or coach may allow you to get to the underlying cause of your behavior and make the required adjustments.

Understanding your attachment type and the attachment style of your spouse is also a terrific self-awareness skill. I regularly suggest the audiobook "Attached" by Amir Levine & Rachel S. F. Heller.

When you sense yourself over-analyzing—you need to shift your attention instantly

I often advise my clients that when you are getting in your head, the easiest way to snap out of it is to concentrate your concentration on something good. When you sense yourself over-analyzing and getting worried, you need to shift your attention instantly.

Go on a stroll, meditate, call a buddy (and chat about anything other than dating), play some fantastic music and dance in your living room, or any other creative outlet you have to alter your mental state.

Practice shifting your attention as soon as you have emotions of insecurity creep up. The more you are consciously aware of it, the better you will get at reframing your thoughts!

Overthinking our personal or professional relationships robs us of creating trust in others, and it dilutes the energy between parties and partners in the present. When you overthink, you generate tension between yourself and other people, assigning meaning to circumstances based on worrying about what you "think" may happen rather than what certainly will occur.

Overthinking the ins and outs of a relationship originates from a scarcity mentality in which you picture a worst-case situation that may never materialize.

Overthinking is based on a concern that a relationship will not work out or be successful. Often, individuals ponder on prior unsuccessful liaisons and transfer anxieties that because a former relationship went poorly, a present connection may as well. This dread and over-analysis may distort and confuse a present relationship and potentially even hinder its progress.

So, what can you do to avoid overthinking if you are in relationship paralysis? Get out of your intellect and into your heart.

Test the veracity of your worries

Test the veracity of your concerns by compiling a list of the worst event that may happen. Then construct a list of the greatest potential result.

This will encourage you in going from overthinking to under-thinking about your relationships. Find a spot in the center of your listings. This will encourage you in powering back on negative thinking and power up on possibilities and abundance.

Plan and commit to events designed to be enjoyed together

When you are involved and engaging with others, it makes it tougher to examine the specifics. Planning and committing to events designed to be enjoyed together generates memories and refocuses your relationships via shared links and enhanced energy.

Communicate with your partner
Shut off negative ideas and noise by asking for what you desire. The more clarity you convey and desire in return, the less overthinking you will do.

Practice gratitude
Keep an ongoing record of your relationship highlights. What makes you smile? What do you appreciate most about this person?

Every morning, begin your day by expressing your thanks for and to others. Thank people who are important to you for being in your life, and be sure to tell them why you value them.

Gratitude helps us to concentrate on the good truths of the intricacies of our relationships which in turn minimizes stress and bad thinking and fosters acceptance.

Identify the cause of the issue

Usually, when individuals overthink, it's because of other underlying concerns. It might be anxiety, despair, OCD, and more that are causing it.

First off, it is vital to discover the core of the issue before it develops into harsher feelings like shutting oneself off, undesired tension, bad thoughts, and even paranoia.

Reflect and concentrate on how you're feeling at the time

Taking time every day to focus on your ideas, objectives, and ideals in life will help you see more clearly. I always advocate journaling. Write it all down. Focus on how you're feeling at the time. Be mindful of your breath, things that pain you, your present thoughts, etc.

Some excellent coaching questions:

How frequently do you make time for yourself?
Are you giving more of yourself than you can take?
Who is there for you?
Check your surroundings
Sometimes, the people, places, or things around us lead us to feel anxiety or heightened negative thoughts. Examining your surroundings might help you locate such "triggers," if there are any.

Some excellent coaching questions:

Is anything or someone making you feel like that?
Who are you surrounding yourself with?
Could something or someone be impacting you but maybe you aren't seeing it?
We have over 50,000 thoughts a day. Mostly those which are bad.

Self-growth is a process that takes time. We can build the life we desire, but it begins with taking the first step and getting assistance.

Get to the root of it

Think at it this way — you're likely not overthinking your connection with other people, so why is it so dead-set focused on your partner?

There's always a reason for anything, but are you prepared to put in the effort for retrospection to assist both of you? In my experience, overthinking has often been due of:

Past traumas

Rumors concerning the new person

A necessity for validation

Fear of the future

Talk to a counselor or even a trusted friend if you're reluctant, and find out what is genuinely causing your excessive concern.

Often, the cause might be a red signal for both of you, so it's preferable to address it from the get-go.

Take the "what if" situations for what they are — a daydream
My customers routinely express concern about prospective future possibilities based on some previous occurrences (and often, no connection at all) and continuously fail to live in the now.

It begins tiny and progressively consumes you whole until you're unable to discern fiction from a plausible reality. The negativity piles up and becomes a poisonous mix that puts a damper on the connection.

Constantly yourself grounded, and keep correcting yourself. Enjoy whatever phase you're in at the moment — whatever is going to happen will happen.

Challenge your preconceptions

Consider this question - would thinking about these uncommon scenarios prevent them? You're not going to be able to enjoy the moment right now, and soon, the paranoia will drive you two to drift apart.

Reprogram your brain. Next time you leap to a conclusion, attempt to conceive of a reasonable explanation and repeat it to yourself until you believe it. 99% of the time, it'll be a regular circumstance that you'll be pleased you didn't descend into.

Communicate and bond more with your spouse

Being a relationship counselor, I have found that one of the causes of breakups is overthinking. Overthinking is like a termite that slowly and gradually damages a relationship.

One may reduce overthinking in a relationship by adopting these helpful tips:

Communicate and connect more with your spouse– Try to keep connected with your partner through messages or brief calls. And if, by chance, your spouse does not respond, then there's no need to overthink. Just go on in your day.

Stop re-reading your spouse's messages – Sometimes, it's important to look over past texts of your partner, particularly during an argument, but ordinary texts don't need a re-read. If a certain text is truly upsetting you then, you may immediately contact your partner to discuss and attempt to figure out how they feel by overthinking.

Stop overanalyzing your partner's body language - In certain circumstances, one could overanalyze their partner's body language; this can be created due to imprecise or no communication between the two. So, instead, a person should go and break the communication gap between them.

Aim for personal satisfaction - Don't feel uneasy or insecure about your relationship. Take out time to start feeling comfortable with yourself.

Build your trust - Trust plays a very major function in a relationship. So if you don't trust your spouse, then don't overthink it. Instead, communicate this concept amongst yourself and start restoring trust.

Try not to take things personally — If your spouse is in a foul mood and said something to you that you thought harsh. Then, no need to take it personally or overthink it since it's not a reflection on you as a person. Also, it doesn't indicate that they don't care about you.

Try to keep occupied and happy - As we know about this common adage that 'an empty mind is a devil's workshop.' So strive to be happy and productive at all times. In order to make things perfect for yourself and your loving partner.\sAddress your negative ideas with replies - When bad thoughts begin to spiral in your head, then it's important for you to confront them by either writing them down or talking to someone. After writing or speaking, you may assess them and then respond properly. Negative ideas might utterly wreck your relationship.

The finest cure is to communicate your opinions with your partner
If you're overthinking about the state of your relationship or questions are coming up about the state of your relationship, the best way to tackle these questions is to get direct answers from your partner.

People are sometimes afraid to share their thoughts with their partners because they're afraid their partner won't respond to them well or are afraid of confrontation or the partner's reaction.

Overthinking in a relationship frequently stems from connection anxiety and uncertainty, when we feel unclear of where we are in a relationship. That's when we tend to obsess and overthink things in a relationship.

At the end of the day, if you don't feel emotionally safe with your partner, it's inevitable that you will be dealing with a lot of overthinking because you don't feel safe enough to share your thoughts with your partner.

Share your views with close friends or family members to assist you to sort out your thoughts

Another technique to manage to overthink is to express your ideas with close friends or family members and have them as a sounding board where they can help you sort out your thoughts and emotions before conveying them to your spouse.

Seek therapy to reduce some of the overthinking

Seeking therapy as side support also helps to reduce some of the overthinking and helps you have greater clarity about where your ideas are coming from and how to handle them.

Replace the ruminating thoughts with thoughts based upon facts and evidence

Overthinking is fueled by rumination, which is a repetitive cycle of obsessive ideas and thoughts. When you ruminate about your relationship, it builds uncertainty. It does not result in a productive outcome.

Rumination creates an experience similar to getting an annoying song stuck in your head that keeps replaying over and over. You feel frustrated, annoyed, and tired because the thoughts don't stop, and it doesn't lead to any resolution. These ideas, and the ensuing unpleasant feelings, weaken your partnership.

So how can you stop ruminating to stop overthinking?

An excellent method is to replace ruminating ideas with concepts based on facts and data. For example, if you keep overthinking whether your spouse cares for you in the same way you care for them, offer your brain the proof.

How does your partner demonstrate they care?
What actions do they do which express their feelings?
Instead of allowing your thoughts to keep spinning, you stop the rumination by identifying the facts to answer the question.

Once you achieve control over the overthinking, it creates room for you to analyze where the dysfunctional thoughts originated from.

Are they residual baggage from earlier relationships?
Are they tied to another aspect of your life in which you have some doubt, and the uncertainty has extended to your relationship?
Once you can understand where the rumination and overthinking started, it provides you more authority to alter the thought pattern when or if it occurs again.

Trust your instincts and carefully take action

Find the reasons why you're overthinking a relationship. Determine whether it's driven by your own fears or if it's because your spouse did something that made you think twice, and now you're overthinking.

Listen to your intuition - what is it saying?

If you honestly think that it's not you and it's your spouse, it will be best to speak to them about what you're experiencing. You must remain strong on your point, however, and help them realize why you're feeling this way — do not put it entirely on them.

Be careful not to gaslight your partner or become aware if you are being gaslighted. Sit it out and respectfully hear each other.

Put the time to focus on the positive
Instead of having worrisome thoughts about the future, reinterpreting the signals constantly, or being irritated with anything they did, invest the time to concentrate on the good no matter how hard it may be for an over-thinker like you.
Be more proactive. If you are confused about anything, ask.

It's a part of the getting to know each other stage. Having misgivings on the commencement of the relationship is acceptable, but never allow it to be the driving force of the connection, otherwise, you are headed to a poisonous start.

Be confident in yourself and trust your spouse
Sometimes, overthinking arises from the concern that “you aren’t enough.”

Trust your spouse; they too are exploring this period as much as you are. You have already come this far, and you have seen each other’s flaws. It’s all a question of realizing that no relationship is flawless, but a successful relationship is established by two individuals who choose to maintain it despite these bumps.

The only way to be here and now is to be present “Happiness is reality minus expectations.”

The more expectations you have, the more you depart from reality, and the more negative you will feel. I advise my clients that using the word 'should'—in mind or vocally is an indication you're racking on expectations.

Another good statement is "Don't 'should' on yourself," and equally, don't 'should' on your spouse or anybody else.

Another beneficial technique to prevent overthinking is the grounding exercise. This mindfulness meditation technique helps individuals be more present at the moment or here and now.

To achieve this job, individuals move from whatever negative notion is distracting them and instead ask themselves:

"What are 5 things I see, 4 things I hear, 3 things I touch, 2 things I smell, and 1 item I taste?"
You can perform any of the senses in any sequence, although some are simpler than others. If this is too hard, you may

substitute it with a shortened version such as “Can I find 5 blue items in this room?” These easy mental exercises bring us out of emotionally overthinking and into a more sensible, cognitive frame of mind.

A good reminder when you are overthinking with either guilt or regret of the past or fear of the future is that sadness originates from a preoccupation with the past, while anxiety comes from an obsession with the future.

Don’t overanalyze their body language
You could keep seeking indicators of problems in your partner’s body language. Unclear communication is a significant factor in overanalyzing things.

Challenge your preconceptions
When you are worried and overthinking, you’re not in the present. This does not enable you to spend time with your lover. If you are not there, how can you improve your relationship?

Focus on personal fulfillment
Your companion may surely make you feel uneasy or hesitant about your connection. However, if everything is smooth and great, and you still feel anxious, try investing that overthinking into yourself.

Ask for guidance less frequently
If you let others influence your relationship, you will have too many views, making it easy to overthink.

Focus on yourself and your satisfaction
The easiest technique to quit overthinking in a relationship is to concentrate on yourself and your satisfaction. If you construct a life that you enjoy, you will automatically quit overthinking. This doesn't happen quickly, but the sooner you start doing this, the better.

You may pursue a new pastime, study a language, establish a fitness goal, or spend time with your pals.

If you love your life on a day-to-day basis, it has various advantages and saves you from overthinking in all aspects, from your relationship to your profession. For starters, you won't overthink since you will have a stronger sense of contentment and feel safer in yourself.

Overthinking arises from insecurity. Plus, because of your improved confidence, your spouse will find you much more appealing. What's hotter than someone who emanates enthusiasm and joy?

Focusing on your contentment may do wonders for a relationship.

It offers you a feeling of independence which is vital for establishing limits in partnerships. Of course, it's also crucial to be thoughtful of your partner's happiness, but living a life that you enjoy will mean that you have more headspace for empathy and compassion towards others as well as yourself. It's ultimately a win-win.

Stop looking into things

You have a chat with your partner, and you start to examine what was said, how they expressed it, their body language, etc. You are delving too deeply into things and begin to persuade yourself some difficulties are not there.

Challenge your preconceptions

Take a step back, ask yourself whether what you are thinking is reasonable, if there's a cause for the emotional responses you are having to the scenario, or if it's anxieties coming out and leading you to overthink.

Stop asking strangers

No one else knows your relationship dynamics other than you and your spouse.

Speak to them about your issues but do not include friends and loved ones who will only receive one side of the story and most likely not help you feel any better.

Don't take things personally
If your spouse looks to be in a foul mood, accept that they are in their mood and allow them to feel the way they do.

Acknowledge that it is not your doing and give them space. Don't take it to heart if they are feeling off and distant on a short-term basis. Their mood will improve, and everything will be good again.

Focus on the good
Always have a list of positives available in case you find yourself sliding into an overthinking attitude where you upset yourself. Having this list is going to remind you that things are excellent and strong and that you are simply fretting for nothing.

A decent exercise may soothe your body, reduce your tension, and clear your thoughts

There is a fantastic adage, "An empty mind is the devil's workshop." This simply implies that if you do not have anything important or helpful to think about, your mind tends to linger or hunt for instant fulfillment.

It has been observed that during times of stress, it is the easiest time to get back into or take up harmful habits/addictions. Now is the moment to quit overthinking everything going on and get engaged in some form of physical exercise.

Contrary to common opinion, the advantages of exercise go well beyond weight reduction and muscle building.

Sports or exercising out may keep your body strong and your mind healthy. A decent exercise may soothe your body, reduce your tension, and cleanse your thoughts. Exercise can enhance your quality of sleep and lessen symptoms of worry and despair.

Studies have shown that exercise may cure moderate depression as successfully as antidepressant drugs. Here are some basic methods to quit overthinking and get moving.

Make a plan

With whatever you undertake, being prepared is the best way to start. Find a time that works best for you, whether it be a fast run to start your day or a workout video to finish it. Not enough time is one of the major reasons individuals claim they cannot work out, therefore you must arrange time into your day.

We squander so much time on our phones or watching TV. If you only take a few minutes away from timewasters, you will notice how simple and rewarding it is to squeeze in a workout.

Make it a habit

It is stated that if you commit to anything for 21-90 days, it will become a habit. So start small and commit to some type of exercise for 21 days.

While it may be scary at first, you will be operating on autopilot in no time. You will want to exercise and feel lethargic if you don't do it. You will begin to feel like your day is incomplete without your regular exercise.

It is crucial to commit and not take days off at the beginning, otherwise, it will take longer for exercise to develop a habit.

Stay motivated

While reducing weight and increasing muscle is a fantastic advantage of exercise, not getting the quick results you seek might be disappointing. Set simple and realistic objectives that will enhance your confidence when you accomplish those milestones.

Remember, not everyone's body is the same. What works for someone else may not be what works best for you. Track your progress. From lifting larger weights to running your mile quicker, progress is a terrific encouragement to keep going.

Be responsible

Working out with a buddy or group can help keep you accountable. You may push each other to get up and go work out. You may also challenge each other to work harder throughout your exercises. Finding a workout class you enjoy is a terrific approach to be responsible. There is a specific time for the lesson that you may arrange into your normal life.

You may also join a team sport. Sports are a terrific method to be responsible since the team depends on each of its players to compete. The competitive element of sports is a terrific way to enhance adrenaline and alleviate stress.

Do what you like

Exercise does not have to be a hassle. There are many methods to exercise so discover what you want to do. If you are a member of a gym, you may try several courses to discover which one you enjoy or do a few to keep it fresh.

Maybe you like riding your bike. If you work close to home, you may replace bringing your bike to work instead of your automobile a couple of days a week. Maybe you are not into strenuous exercises; try something more calming like yoga.

Exercise is not a one size fits all answer, so determine what works best for you. The more you appreciate something, the more inclined you are to do it.

If you are new to working out, there are a few points to remember:

Stay hydrated

Hydrating is vital when working out. Not drinking enough water might cause you to cramp up and not feel well overall. Water or Gatorade that contains electrolytes can aid maintain maximum performance during your exercise.

Also, remaining hydrated after your exercise can help you recuperate and be ready for your next session.

Warm-up

When you are ready to exercise, it is vital to warm up. This can assist avoid injuries and getting the most out of your activity. Stretching and warming up can also decrease feeling sore after your exercise and may assist improve your flexibility.

If you are planning to go for a run, start with a stretch and a little walk before you begin jogging. If you are lifting weights, work your way up to the larger weights to warm your muscles up.

Listen to your body

Know your boundaries, and do not push yourself too much. Working out quicker or harder does not imply better exercise. Take your time and take breaks as required. Pushing too hard is the quickest way to damage oneself.

Cooldown

Just as it is vital to warm up, cooling down is equally crucial. Cooling down reduces your heart rate and respiration back to normal levels. It also helps to relieve discomfort after a workout. The objective of the cool-down time is to restore your body to its natural condition.

There are several methods to occupy your thoughts and help you avoid overthinking any relationship issues, but exercise is a terrific diversion. It is excellent for both your mind and body. It is a good habit that you may acquire to assist engage you and get away from your usual stress.

Relationships may be thrilling, especially when they are fresh. You could have plenty of thrilling sensations as well as loads of anxieties regarding the state of this new connection. It might be tempting to overthink every stage of this new relationship, just as it can be easy to overthink everything when you are in an established relationship.

Humans are naturally predisposed to search for issues. It is encoded into our DNA and is tied to our urge to seek problems that can harm our safety and survival. While we would assume that these sorts of instincts and hardwiring do not alter our view of the events in our life, these internal emotions and sentiments might be partially beyond our control.

If you are battling with overthinking and believe it impacts your relationship, read on for some assistance with this common issue.

Enjoy the present moment

It may be easy to start thinking about the next stages of your relationship, especially if you are highly interested in the person or if you have been dating a long and believe that it might be time for the next steps. However, this is not a practical technique for judging the progress of a relationship.

While you may have specific requirements that are not being fulfilled and need to address them with your spouse, you should try not to worry over the timeframes that you want the relationship to follow.

You will discover that there is no guidebook for what is "normal" in any relationship, and becoming agitated over thoughts that yours is not on track will merely make you worried.

Be honest about your emotions

Sometimes the greatest method to overcome emotions of uneasiness or uncertainties is to just speak about them. Unless you are inside the first few dates of a new relationship, you should be able to voice issues or concerns to the individual so that they may be handled. Being able to bring an internal stressor out into the open might help eliminate it for good.

The second advantage of being honest about your feelings in a relationship is that your spouse may react to you and express their own emotions or worries. You could realize that you are experiencing the same things and be able to reject these anxieties together!

Being honest with the other person is a significant part in good relationships, and there is no better time than the present to start being open with the person you are seeing.

Take a step back and look at your relationship with an objective eye

If you discover that your sentiments are spinning and you're making plenty of assumptions, it might be good to take a step back and look at your relationship with an objective eye.

Sometimes our moods and fears make us see things that are not there to view. You can be anxious about something that has not taken occurred, and when you take a step back, you should be able to realize that this is the case.

Looking at the facts relating to your relationship is always a lot more beneficial than examining your anxieties and worries as they are truly facts. Being able to take a step away from your relationship to take a look at it with fresh eyes may help you check the facts of your relationship with a clear brain.

Focus on your fulfillment

It might be easy to want your spouse to make you happy and meet all your hopes and objectives for the ideal relationship. This is not realistic in many respects, though, and you can discover that even a terrific relationship can be wrecked by your aspirations for personal satisfaction inside the partnership.

At the end of the day, you have to be happy for yourself too, and you cannot expect your relationship to make you happy regularly.

If you discover that you are leaning on your relationship for all of your requirements for personal satisfaction, this can end up causing you distress. You should not forget your demands for personal satisfaction relating to hobbies, time spent doing things alone, and taking the time to make sure that you are comfortable with yourself.

You cannot forget to take care of yourself simply because you are focused on your relationship.

Be wary about asking for advice

While it might be tempting to unload your problems and concerns to friends and family, occasionally their participation in your relationship is not beneficial at all.

Other people may perceive your relationship through a lens that is not realistic, and their advice could just deepen your emotions of fear and stress. It may be beneficial in certain cases to seek outside advice pertaining to your relationship, but at the end of the day, you know best what is going on in this section of your life.

Sometimes, outside forces might instill fears in your head that are unneeded. They may also contribute to your general anxieties about the connection rather than helping to alleviate them. Having other people involved in your relationship may also lead to bad emotions and turmoil that might have been avoided by talking to your spouse directly about your feelings.

Always remember that you should not become irritated at yourself for overthinking your relationship. This is part of human nature. Use these suggestions to manage your expectations and fears linked to your relationship and take time to meditate or objectively examine your relationship as required.

Managing your emotions and your fears linked to any relationship may be tricky at first, but as you grow better at analyzing the situation with these techniques in mind, you will find that you feel less concerned and less nervous.

Relationships require work, both within and outwardly, but they are well worth this effort.

Chapter 5

What a healthy partnership should resemble

Romantic relationships may be incredibly hard work! Whether you've just met or you've been together for a long, it may be hard to tell from the inside whether your relationship is healthy. And if you have a very problematic background with relationships, it might be much more difficult.

This is particularly true when you're in the honeymoon period of your relationship. If you're in a new relationship, you undoubtedly view your spouse through a set of rose-colored glasses. You could perceive them as the most amazing, ideal person in the world.

Rose-colored glasses make it more difficult to discern whether your relationship is healthy or not. This remark from BoJack Horseman says it quite well:

"When you look at someone through rose-colored glasses, all the red flags simply seem like flags."

Ignoring warning signals and ending up in a toxic relationship may do some big harm to your mental health. It's crucial to know what a good relationship is like so that you don't find yourself in a poisonous scenario.

So what does a healthy relationship look like? Not every relationship looks the same. However, several clear symptoms might help you discover whether your is healthy. Here are a few Signs of a good relationship
You trust each other
When you're in a healthy relationship, you have to be able to trust one other. This

involves trusting them with things like being loyal, spending money, and making parental choices.

Without a feeling of trust, there's no sense of security. That implies there's no firm basis for you to create a healthy relationship.

Your life doesn't revolve around each other

Both your relationship and your mental health must have a life and identity of your own. That includes not losing your friends, hobbies, or interests simply because you're in a relationship.

Your relationship is designed to enrich your life, not become your life. There's a notion that your spouse is expected to 'complete' you. Believing that may lead to harmful and codependent relationships.

You interact freely and honestly with each other

Being able to open up to one another is a crucial aspect of any good relationship. This includes feeling secure to speak about what's going on in your life and topics that are on your mind.

This might take a while. Your spouse may not comprehend your communication style immediately away, and vice versa. Dr. Gary Chapman, the author of The 5 Love Languages, recommends sometimes it takes a little time to understand and adapt to how your spouse talks and hears love.

You're comfortable with one another

Being able to be yourself with your spouse is a positive indicator that they are welcoming and that your connection is strong.

Do you find yourself walking on eggshells or being uncomfortable and worried around your partner? That may be your body notifying you that there's something wrong.

You manage and overcome conflict jointly

Just because you're in a good relationship doesn't imply that you'll never quarrel. In reality, every good relationship contains conflict. Being able to manage disagreement well with your spouse is a positive indicator of a healthy dynamic.

This implies that when you and your spouse quarrel, you manage it together as a team.

You handle the problem jointly and find a method to compromise with one another.

You keep the closeness alive

Physical closeness like sex or snuggling is crucial in a relationship. This might alter over time, but making sure you're keeping that component of your relationship alive is important to being in a healthy relationship. You should also maintain the emotional connection alive in your partnership. This might look like checking in with each other often or doing meaningful things together. Or, it may mean attempting something new together.

You spend a decent amount of time together

It's crucial to keep your personality outside of your relationship. Yet, it doesn't imply that you have to conduct wholly distinct lifestyles.

Being in a healthy relationship requires spending quality time with one another. You may go on frequent date evenings, work out together, or plan a vacation together.

You respect one another

Respect is a very vital aspect of being in a good relationship. Respect might entail creating healthy interpersonal boundaries with one another. It also entails respecting those limits when they are enforced.

It may also entail accepting each other's differences and needs. This includes not denigrating or disparaging your spouse to their face or behind their back.

You're friendly and fun with one another

Who wants to be in a dull relationship? If you can joke about and be lighthearted with one other, it's a terrific indicator that your relationship is on good footing.

Sharing lighthearted moments and being affectionate with one another may help you create a solid relationship and enhance your connection.

You're interested in each other's life

Being truly inquisitive about your spouse and their ideas, hopes, desires, or routine everyday tasks is a solid indicator that you're in a good connection.

This goes both ways. Your companion should be interested in your ideas, wishes, desires, or whatever makes you tick.
It might be hard to tell from the inside if you're in a healthy relationship. But, these indications are a wonderful place to start.

If you're experiencing relationship troubles, it might benefit to undertake solo treatment before completing couples counseling. Sometimes we transfer old relationship experiences into our present one without recognizing it. Working with a therapist on your own might help you process them. Even if you're in a stable relationship, attending an individual therapist may help you build communication and conflict resolution skills. They may function as an objective observer and provide you an impartial view on your relationship that your friends or family couldn't give you. They may also help you see if you or your partner are demonstrating healthy limits in relationships.

Chapter 6

How to establish a healthy relationship

All romantic relationships go through ups and downs and they all involve effort, dedication, and a desire to adapt and evolve alongside your spouse. But whether your relationship is just starting or you've been together for years, there are actions you can do to establish a healthy connection. Even if you've suffered several unsuccessful relationships in the past or have battled previously to reignite the embers of passion in your present relationship, you may discover strategies to remain connected, find contentment, and enjoy enduring happiness.

What constitutes a healthy relationship?

Every relationship is unique, and individuals come together for many different reasons. Part of what constitutes a good relationship is having a clear aim for precisely what you want the relationship to be and where you want it to go. And that's something you'll only know through discussing truly and honestly with your spouse.

However, there are also several features that most good partnerships have in common. Knowing these fundamental concepts will help maintain your relationship engaging, rewarding, and exciting whatever objectives you're working towards or obstacles you're experiencing together.

You keep a genuine emotional connection with each other. You each make the other feel cherished and emotionally satisfied. There's a difference between being loved and feeling loved. When you feel loved, it helps you feel welcomed and cherished by your relationship, like someone genuinely understands you. Some relationships become caught in peaceful cohabitation, but without the parties genuinely responding to one other emotionally. While the partnership may look secure on the surface, a lack of continual commitment and emotional connection works merely to increase the distance between two individuals.

You're not frightened of (respectful) disagreement. Some couples hash things out softly, while others may raise their voices and strongly dispute. The key to a successful relationship, however, is not to be scared of disputes. You need to feel comfortable sharing things that upset you without fear of reprisal and be able to settle a dispute without shame, degradation, or insistence on being right.

You keep outside contacts and interests alive.

Despite the boasts of romantic novels or movies, no one person can fulfill all of your requirements. Demanding too much from your spouse may impose harmful strain on a relationship. To excite and deepen your love relationship, it's necessary to keep your own identity outside of the partnership, preserve relationships with family and friends, and maintain your hobbies and interests.

You communicate frankly and honestly. Good communication is a fundamental aspect of every relationship. When both individuals know what they want from the relationship and feel comfortable expressing their wants, worries, and desires, it may enhance trust and improve the link between you.

Falling in love vs. remaining in love

For most individuals, falling in love generally appears to simply happen. It's staying in love—or retaining that "falling in love" experience—that demands dedication and labor. Given its benefits, however, it's definitely worth the effort. A solid, safe romantic relationship may serve as a continual source of support and satisfaction in your life, through good times and bad, boosting all elements of your wellness. By taking efforts today to maintain or reignite your falling-in-love experience, you may develop a meaningful connection that lasts—even for a lifetime.

Many couples concentrate on their relationship only when there are definite, inevitable challenges to solve. Once the difficulties have been handled they frequently move their focus back to their work, kids, or other hobbies. However, romantic partnerships need continual care and commitment for love to grow. As long as the health of a romantic connection is vital to you, it is going to need your attention and work. And detecting and addressing a tiny issue in your relationship now may frequently help avoid it from turning into a much bigger one down the road.

The following recommendations might enable you to retain the falling in love sensation and keep your romantic connection healthy.

Tip 1: *Spend meaningful time face to face*
You fall in love gazing at and listening to each other. If you continue to look and listen in the same attentive manner, you may prolong the falling-in-love experience over the long term. You undoubtedly have wonderful recollections of when you were initially dating your loved one. Everything

felt fresh and wonderful, and you likely spent hours simply conversing together or coming up with new, fascinating things to try. However, as time goes by, the pressures of the job, family, other commitments, and the desire we all have for time to ourselves may make it difficult to find time together.

Many couples discover that the face-to-face interaction of their early dating days is progressively supplanted by hasty texts, emails, and instant messaging. While digital communication is useful for certain reasons, it doesn't favorably affect your brain and nervous system in the same manner as face-to-face conversation. Sending a text or a voice message to your spouse saying "I love you" is nice, but if you seldom look at them or have the opportunity to sit down with them, they'll still believe you don't understand or respect them. And you'll grow more alienated or disengaged as a pair. The emotional signals you both need to feel loved can only be transmitted in person, so no matter how hectic life becomes, it's crucial to carve out time to spend together. Commit to spending some quality time together regularly. No matter how busy you are, spend a few minutes each day to lay away your technological gadgets, stop thinking about other things, and genuinely concentrate on and connect with your spouse.

Find something that you like doing together, whether it be a common activity, dancing class, daily stroll, or relaxing over a cup of coffee in the morning.

Try something new together. Doing new activities together may be a wonderful way to connect and keep things fresh. It might be as easy as trying a new restaurant or going on a day trip to an area you've never visited before.

Focus on having fun together. Couples are frequently more fun and lighthearted in the early stages of a relationship. However, this fun approach may often be lost when real obstacles start getting in the way or old resentments start piling up. Keeping a sense of humor might really help you get through challenging times, decrease stress and work through challenges more readily. Think of amusing ways to surprise your lover, like bringing flowers home or unexpectedly scheduling a table at their favorite restaurant. Playing with dogs or little children may also help you reconnect with your playful side.

Do activities together that help others

One of the most effective methods of keeping close and connected is to jointly concentrate on something you and your spouse appreciate outside of the relationship. Volunteering for a cause, project, or community activity that has importance for both of you may keep a relationship new and intriguing. It may also expose you both to new people and ideas, give the opportunity to face new difficulties together, and provide fresh ways of communicating with each other.

As well as helping to ease stress, worry, and depression, doing things to assist others gives enormous joy. Human people are hard-wired to aid others. The more you contribute, the better you'll feel——as individuals and as a pair.

Tip 2: *Stay engaged via conversation*
Good communication is a crucial aspect of a good relationship. When you have a good emotional connection with your spouse, you feel secure and joyful. When individuals stop communicating properly, they stop

interacting well, and times of transition or stress may especially bring out the separation. It may seem basic, but as long as you are speaking, you can typically work through any challenges you're encountering.

Tell your spouse what you need, don't let them guess.

It's not always simple to speak about what you need. For one, many of us don't spend enough time thinking about what's essential to us in a relationship. And even if you do know what you need, talking about it might make you feel vulnerable, humiliated, or even ashamed. But look at it from your partner's point of view. Providing comfort and understanding to someone you love is a joy, not a responsibility.

If you've known one other for a time, you may believe that your partner has a very decent notion of what you are thinking and what you need. However, your companion is not a mind-reader. While your spouse may have some notion, it is much better to explain your desires clearly to prevent any misunderstanding.

Your spouse may detect something, but it may not be what you need. What's more, individuals evolve, and what you needed and desired five years ago, for example, may be completely different today. So instead of allowing frustration, confusion, or rage to build when your spouse consistently gets it wrong, get in the practice of telling them precisely what you need.

Take attention to your partner's nonverbal clues

So much of our communication is communicated by what we don't say. Nonverbal signals, which include eye contact, tone of voice, posture, and gestures such as leaning forward, crossing your arms, or touching someone's hand, transmit considerably more than words.

When you can pick up on your partner's nonverbal clues or "body language," you'll be able to determine how they genuinely feel and be able to react properly. For a relationship to operate properly, each individual needs to understand their own and their partner's nonverbal clues. Your partner's answers may be different from yours. For example, one person could find a hug after a difficult day a loving way of communication—while another would simply want to take a stroll together or sit and converse.

It's also crucial to make sure that what you say fits your body language. If you say "I'm fine," but you clench your teeth and turn away, then your body is suggesting you are everything but "fine."

When you perceive good emotional signals from your relationship, you feel cherished and joyful, and when you transmit positive emotional cues, your partner feels the same. When you cease taking an interest in your own or your partner's feelings, you'll weaken the connection between you, and your ability to communicate will decrease, particularly during difficult situations.

Be a good listener

While a great lot of emphasis in our culture is focused on talking, if you can learn to listen in a manner that makes another person feel appreciated and understood, you may establish a deeper, stronger connection between you.

There's a tremendous difference between listening in this manner and merely hearing. When you truly listen—when you're engaged with what's being said—you'll notice the tiny intonations in your partner's voice that inform you how they're feeling and the emotions they're attempting to transmit. Being a good listener doesn't mean you have to agree with your spouse or alter your views. But it will help you uncover shared points of view that may allow you to overcome disputes.

Manage stress

When you're anxious or emotionally overloaded, you're more prone to misjudge your romantic partner, give confused or off-putting nonverbal signals, or slip into dangerous knee-jerk patterns of behavior. How often have you been anxious and gone off the handle at your loved one and said or done something you afterward regretted?

If you can learn to rapidly handle tension and return to a calm condition, you'll not only prevent such regrets, but you'll also help to avoid conflict and misunderstandings——and even help to calm your spouse when tempers mount.

Tip 3: *Keep physical intimacy alive*
Touch is an essential component of human life. Studies on babies have proven the value of frequent, loving interaction for brain development. And the advantages don't stop in childhood. Affectionate touch enhances the body's levels of oxytocin, a hormone that promotes bonding and attachment.

While sex is frequently a cornerstone of a committed relationship, it shouldn't be the primary way of physical closeness. Frequent, loving touch—holding hands, embracing, kissing—is equally crucial.

Of course, it's crucial to be attentive to what your spouse enjoys. Unwanted touching or improper approaches might make the other person stiffen up and retreat—exactly what you don't want. As with so many other parts of a successful relationship, this might come down to how effectively you express your wants and intentions with your spouse.

Even if you have urgent responsibilities or small children to think about, you can assist to keep physical intimacy alive by carving out some regular couple time, whether that's in the shape of a date night or just an hour at the end of the day when you can sit and speak or hold hands.

Tip 4: *Learn to give and take in your relationship*

If you expect to obtain what you want 100% of the time in a relationship, you are setting yourself up for disappointment. Healthy relationships are founded on compromise. However, it requires effort on each person's side to make sure that there is a fair exchange.

Recognize what's essential to your partner

Knowing what is important to your spouse may go a long way towards developing goodwill and an attitude of compromise. On the other side, it's as crucial for your spouse to notice your desires and for you to voice them properly. Constantly giving to others at the cost of your own needs can only generate resentment and bitterness.

Don't make "winning" your aim

If you approach your spouse with the mindset that things have to be your way or else, it will be tough to find a compromise. Sometimes this attitude stems from not having your needs addressed when younger, or it might be years of collected animosity in the relationship reaching a boiling point. It's okay to have strong opinions about something, but your spouse needs to be heard as well. Be courteous of the other person and their views.

Learn how to politely settle a disagreement

Conflict is unavoidable in every relationship, but to keep a relationship healthy, both individuals need to feel they've been heard. The objective is not to win but to retain and grow the connection.

Make sure you are battling fair. Keep the focus on the matter at hand and respect the other person. Don't start debates about things that cannot be altered.

Don't insult someone directly but use "I" phrases to explain how you feel. For example, instead of stating, "You make me feel horrible" try "I feel bad when you do that".

Don't draw previous disagreements into the mix. Rather than turning to previous battles or grudges and assigning blame, concentrate on what you can do in the here-and-now to remedy the situation.

Be willing to forgive. Resolving conflict is difficult if you're unwilling or unable to forgive people.

If tempers flare, take a break. Take a few minutes to reduce tension and cool down before you say or do anything you'll regret. Always remember that you're fighting with the person you love.

Know when to let things go. If you can't come to an agreement, agree to disagree. It takes two individuals to keep an argument going. If a fight is going nowhere, you might opt to withdraw and go on.

Tip 5: Be prepared for ups and downs

It's crucial to remember that there are ups and downs in any relationship. You won't always be on the same page. Sometimes one spouse may be coping with an event that concerns them, such as the loss of a close family member. Other circumstances, including job loss or significant health difficulties, might impact both couples and make it difficult to connect with each other. You can have different notions about managing funds or parenting children.

Different individuals handle stress differently, and misconceptions may easily develop into irritation and fury.

Don't take out your issues on your spouse. Life stressors might make us short-tempered. If you are managing a lot of stress, it could seem simpler to vent with your spouse, and perhaps seem safer to snap at them. Fighting like this can first seem like a release, but it progressively ruins your relationship. Find alternative better methods to handle your stress, anger, and irritation.

Trying to impose a solution might produce even more complications. Every individual works with challenges and concerns in their manner. Remember that you're a team. Continuing to move ahead together might help you through the hard periods.

Look back to the early phases of your relationship. Share the events that brought the two of you together, evaluate the point at which you started to drift apart, and determine how you may work together to restore that falling-in-love experience.

Be open to change. Change is inevitable in life, and it will happen whether you go with it or oppose it. Flexibility is vital to adjust to the change that is continually going place in every relationship, and it helps you to develop together through both the good times and the bad.

If you need outside aid for your relationship, seek it out jointly. Sometimes difficulties in a relationship might feel too complicated or overwhelming for you to manage as a pair. Couples' counseling or discussing jointly with a trustworthy friend or religious figure may assist.

www.ingramcontent.com/pod-product-compliance
Lightning Source LLC
LaVergne TN
LVHW010609160826
845677LV00013B/3326

* 9 7 9 8 8 4 7 4 0 5 4 3 0 *